Authentic Volpi

The original Volpi salami processing and curing room, circa 1910.

When Giovanni Volpi left Milan for America in 1900, he was in search of adventure and the bold promise of the American Dream. In Italy, he had been a gifted salumiere—a master in making salami, prosciutto, and other dry-cured meats. In America, he would transplant his love for his craft and its Old World traditions to the rich heartland of his adopted country.

A dedication to his profession, combined with the bountiful harvest of the Midwest, allowed him to recreate the treasured cured meats of his native Italy in the Italian immigrant neighborhood of St. Louis known as The Hill.

From his storefront in this thriving community, Uncle John began what would become one of the world's premier dry-cured meats companies—one steeped in the traditions of the Old World yet mindful of the innovations of the New World.

As you enjoy the recipes, anecdotes, and histories in *Authentic Volpi*, we encourage you to follow the story of John Volpi and Company and the families whose passions made this all possible.

Authentic Volpi

By Sarah Kellogg and Chef Michael Laukert

with Lorenza Pasetti

Illustrations by Marsha Lederman

REEDY PRESS

St. Louis, Missouri

Reedy Press
PO Box 5131
St. Louis, MO 63139
www.reedypress.com

design by Lynne Smyers

Library of Congress Cataloging-in-Publication Data: 2009938061

ISBN: 978-1-933370-50-7

Printed in the United States
09 10 11 12 13   5 4 3 2 1

Table of Contents

Introduction

Like my father and great uncles before me, I proudly call myself a salumiere—steadfastly committed to making premium Italian-style, dry-cured meats, and to selling these exceptional products here and around the globe.

As a child, I first learned about the curing process by walking through our aromatic wooden curing rooms. As a teenager, I discovered Volpi's popularity on summer afternoons with my sister, Vivian, as we packaged salami for distribution to distant cities.

When I joined my father, Armando Pasetti, in the business as an adult, it was with a deep understanding of the company's role in our lives and the importance of doing only my best work for our loyal customers and valued staff.

These many years later, I have watched my own children grow up at Volpi, and I feel even more profoundly the legacy that has passed from one generation to the next for more than a century.

With that legacy in mind, we decided to create *Authentic Volpi*. We favored an almanac, with its informality and informational focus, as a way of sharing our history and favorite recipes. To complete the enterprise, we turned to Sarah Kellogg and Chef Michael Laukert.

A talented writer, Sarah is also a longtime friend, and she ably came aboard to guide the almanac's production. As a journalist, freelance writer, and editor, she led a gifted team of professionals to create the almanac.

Michael is an experienced hand in the kitchen, and his discerning knowledge of flavor combinations, food history, and gourmet cooking made him a perfect choice to assist us in creating and updating recipes. You can sample his insights into cooking on his blog on our website (volpifoods.com) and in the individual recipe introductions in this almanac.

With *Authentic Volpi*, we happily introduce you to John Volpi and Company, its long history of making dry-cured meats, and the joy that comes with sharing a delicious meal with family and friends. *Buongusto*!

Lorenza Pasetti
St. Louis, Missouri

Foreword

As a chef, some of the most meaningful moments in my life and work have come from the deep and abiding connections I've made with people over a good meal. That is especially true of my bond with the Pasetti family.

In April 2005, I first met Lorenza Pasetti and her father, Armando Pasetti, in the upstairs offices of Uno, the spiritual and physical home of John Volpi and Company for much of its 107 years. The walls were adorned with photos of family members and important milestones in Volpi history.

That afternoon, Armando shared memories of his childhood, his family, and the Volpi business, which he has nurtured for more than 60 years. In these experiences, I found the depth and flavor of the Volpi story, one rich with passionate traditions and a practiced dedication to craft.

I feel this cookbook is the culmination of those conversations. It highlights a family whose history and traditions in the world of Italian cured meats are second to none in the United States.

Our recipes illustrate how Italian cured meats can find a home outside of the traditional antipasto platter. In its simplest form, a piece of Volpi Prosciutto or a slice of Volpi Genova Salame represents the truest form of craftsmanship.

In organizing this book, the concept of seasonality was a unifying theme. Buying seasonally is a prime tenet of the Volpi culinary philosophy, and mine as well. As a chef, my goal is always to start with the finest ingredients, and most often the finest ingredients are the freshest. Ripe fruits and vegetables are at their flavor peak, and their maturity allows us to play off their complex flavors during cooking. By honoring the abundance of the earth and marrying our cooking repertoire with the harvest calendar, amateur and professional chefs alike can create simple yet great meals.

From our families to yours, we wish you good cooking and good times. *Buon appetito*!

Chef Michael Laukert
Colorado Springs, Colorado

Authentic Volpi

When spring first stirs, the lush green of summer is little more than a promise. Faint signs of winter's end come initially in colors, with the arrival of the vibrant-hued crocus, daffodil, and azalea, and then the early lettuces come bursting forth in great bundles of green. This is where prosciutto, bresaola, and pancetta first show themselves worthy rivals for the chef's heart. Their subtle flavors are easily wedded to the tenderness of early peas, spinach, and asparagus, and their versatility ensures their supporting role in the home kitchen throughout the year.

Spring

Poached Egg with Crispy Volpi Pancetta on Pugliese with Mixed Greens and Blue Cheese

This dish makes for a deliciously different, light weekend lunch or a festive holiday brunch. Add a mixed melon cup and enjoy.

Ingredients

4 cups water

I tsp white distilled vinegar

6 large eggs

12 thin slices Volpi Pancetta

6 cups spring mixed greens — rinsed and dried, loosely packed

1/3 pound blue cheese, crumbled

2 Tbsp extra-virgin olive oil

1½ tsp balsamic vinegar

sea salt to taste

black pepper to taste, freshly ground

6 slices pugliese or other hard-crusted bread, sliced ½-inch thick

2 Tbsp butter, unsalted

Serves 6

Pugliese (pool-yee-ay'-zee) – A hearth bread that hails from Puglia, Italy's geographic boot heel

Cooking Method

Preheat oven to 400° F. Place sliced pugliese on sheet pan and place in the oven until lightly toasted, approx. 3 minutes each side. Once toasted, remove and apply a light coating of butter. Set aside and keep warm.

Gently place the Volpi Pancetta on a non-stick baking sheet pan, keeping the pinwheel shape intact. Place in the oven and cook until golden brown and crispy, 10 to 12 minutes. Remove from oven, place on paper towel, and keep warm.

Begin to poach the eggs (*see poaching directions below*). During the poaching process, continue preparations. Place one piece of toasted pugliese on serving plates; place two pieces of the cooked Volpi Pancetta on top.

Toss mixed greens in a medium mixing bowl. Drizzle with olive oil and balsamic vinegar; season with salt and pepper to taste. Divide greens evenly on each plate and garnish with crumbled blue cheese.

Place egg on top of each slice of bread. Lightly season eggs with salt and pepper. Serve immediately.

The Art of Egg Poaching

Poaching eggs is more art than science, so it's important to have a few tricks up your sleeve. One of those is using a shallow cup to speed the process. Crack an egg into a shallow cup and place the cup in the boiling water. Using tongs, gently slide the egg from the cup into the water. When the water returns to boiling, reduce heat to simmer, allowing the egg to set. A perfect egg combines a soft yolk and firm white. Remember to dry each egg before serving.

Volpi Rotola Frittata

This Italian skillet omelet makes a delightful dinner on a cozy spring evening. Dress it up with mixed greens and hearty Italian bread toasted to perfection.

Ingredients

10 brown eggs, fresh
1 package Volpi Rotola, sliced ½-inch thick
1 cup diced potatoes, boiled
1 tomato, diced
½ green pepper, diced
¼ cup Italian parsley — fresh, chopped
2 large scallions, diced diagonally
½ cup mushrooms, cooked
1 Tbsp butter
1 oz extra-virgin olive oil

Serves 6

Frittata (freet-tah´-tah) – Eggs mixed with vegetables, meat, or cheese

Cooking Method

Scramble eggs in large bowl. Add all ingredients to eggs except Volpi Rotola. Save some parsley for garnish before serving.

Using 2 large skillets, add olive oil and a little butter to grease all sides of pan. Heat well; add mixture. Split between 2 skillets. Top the egg mixture in each skillet with layers of Volpi Rotola slices. Turn egg mixture once by placing an inverted dish over skillet. Cook an additional 3 to 5 minutes. Lower heat; turn frittata onto plate and cut into wedges.

Our History | VOLPI | 1905–1930
THE TASTE OF ITALY SINCE 1902

Uncle John and his wife, Maria, were soon joined by Maria's brother, Gino Pasetti. Gino came to America to work in the business, and the two men swiftly earned a reputation among their fellow immigrants for a commitment to Old World traditions and tastes. As their fame and business grew, the ambitious men began to sell salami beyond the confines of The Hill neighborhood. By 1925, they responded to the growing interest in their products by expanding the production facility and adding new product lines to meet the increasing demand for dry-cured meats.

Roasted Asparagus and Volpi Prosciutto with Pine Nut Gremolata

This recipe effortlessly combines two of Italian cooking's most lively trimmings—pine nuts and gremolata, a finely chopped mixture that is used as a topping to brighten any dish.

Ingredients

1 Tbsp butter, unsalted
1½ pounds asparagus – blanched for 2 to 3 minutes (*al dente*)
3 Tbsp extra-virgin olive oil
12 thin slices Volpi Prosciutto
sea salt to taste
black pepper to taste, freshly ground

Pine Nut Gremolata

2 Tbsp pine nuts – toasted, finely chopped
3 Tbsp breadcrumbs – toasted, finely ground
1½ Tbsp Italian parsley, finely minced
3 tsp lemon zest, freshly grated
sea salt to taste
black pepper to taste, freshly ground

Serves 6

Pinolo (pee-noh'-lo) – Pine nut

Cooking Method

Preheat oven to 400° F. Lightly butter a baking dish for the asparagus bundles. Set aside. Season blanched asparagus with olive oil, salt, and pepper. Separate into 6 even piles.

On a cutting board, slightly overlap two pieces of Volpi Prosciutto. Neatly place the asparagus atop the Volpi Prosciutto; carefully roll up to create bundles. Place inside the baking dish and cook for approx. 10 minutes. Asparagus should be tender and the Volpi Prosciutto crispy.

Pine Nut Gremolata

In a mixing bowl, combine all ingredients and mix well. Yield: approx. ½ cup. The asparagus and Volpi Prosciutto can be served in the baking dish or on a serving platter. Garnish each with pine nut gremolata before serving.

In Search of the Perfect Asparagus

To select quality asparagus, look for a vibrant green spear with small, tight leaves at the tip. Asparagus can be thick or thin, depending on when the spears are harvested. To prep, snap off the tough end of one spear, and use this as a guide to cut the remaining spears. Having the asparagus all one length will ensure proper cooking and create an appealing presentation. To blanch asparagus, drop the spears in a large pot of rapidly boiling, salted water, and leave for 3 minutes. Place on a towel-lined sheet to allow for cooling.

Orecchiette with Volpi Pancetta and Chives

With its handful of basic ingredients and ease of preparation, this dish exemplifies the simplicity of Italian food.

Ingredients

1 pound orecchiette pasta
8 oz Volpi Pancetta, sliced and cut into ½-inch lardons
1 tsp extra-virgin olive oil
4 Tbsp butter, unsalted
3 Tbsp chives, minced
½ cup parmesan cheese, large ribbon-cut
black pepper to taste, freshly ground

Serves 4–6

Orecchiette (oar-reh-kee-et´-tay) – A type of pasta shaped like an ear; in Italian, ear is "orecchio"

Cooking Method

Bring a large pot of well-salted water to a boil. Add pasta and cook until *al dente*, 10 to 12 minutes.

While the pasta is cooking, add olive oil to a large sauté pan over medium-high heat. Once hot, add Volpi Pancetta, reduce heat to medium, and allow it to render and caramelize, 10 to 12 minutes. During the final 1 to 2 minutes of cooking, add butter.

Once butter has melted, place 4 oz of the pasta water into the sauté pan and bring to a simmer; then reduce liquid by 50 percent.

Drain the pasta, reserving a small amount of the water to adjust the pasta sauce consistency, if necessary. Add pasta to the sauté pan and toss well. Add chives and adjust seasonings as necessary.

Place in serving bowls, garnish with ribbons of parmesan cheese, and serve.

Chef's tip: To create ribbons of parmesan, utilize a vegetable peeler.

Salumi: Italy's Gift to the World

The word "salumi" is a universal term used to describe cured meats in two categories: *stagionati*, aged cuts of whole-muscle meat, and *insaccati*, ground meat stuffed in casings. While most salumi are made from pork, they also can have beef, goose, and turkey as their bases. Salumi mature in aromatic curing rooms, hanging from wooden poles. Salumi are often named after the regions or cities of their origin, such as Genoa or Milano. Geography frequently influences their flavors, as artisans use popular regional spices such as garlic, paprika, or chili powder to create distinctive flavors.

Frittata with Volpi Coppa, Spring Onion, and Pepper

This is one of those comfort foods that can be enjoyed in any season. Frittata dishes allow for endless creativity in the pairing of savory ingredients.

Ingredients

8 large eggs
½ cup spring onions – thinly sliced, approx. ⅛-inch
½ cup red bell pepper, small dice
3 oz Volpi Coppa – sliced, then small dice
2 Tbsp butter, unsalted
¼ cup milk
2 tsp Italian parsley – fresh, chopped
½ cup parmesan cheese, grated
1 tsp sea salt
¼ tsp black pepper, freshly ground

Serves 4–6

Pepe nero (pep´-pey ney´-roh) – Black pepper

Cooking Method

———•••••◆⧼◆⧽◆•••••———

Preheat broiler, place top rack 6 to 8 inches below the broiler element.

Place 1 Tbsp butter in a non-stick sauté pan over medium heat. As butter melts, add the diced Volpi Coppa and cook for 1 to 2 minutes to develop slight color. Add peppers and spring onions; season with ½ tsp salt and ⅛ tsp pepper. Cook for 7 to 10 minutes. Once vegetables are tender, remove from pan and let cool.

While the vegetables cool, whisk eggs and milk together and season with remaining salt and pepper. Add parsley and parmesan; mix well. Once the Volpi Coppa, spring onions, and red bell peppers are cool, add the egg mixture.

Melt remaining butter in non-stick sauté pan using medium heat. Once pan is hot, add egg mixture and stir well. Using a circular motion, stir the egg mixture a few times during this stage of cooking, 1 to 2 minutes. Leave egg mixture to set, approx. 5 minutes. Move the sauté pan to the broiler, 3 to 5 minutes.

Once frittata is golden brown, remove from oven and allow to cool. Frittata will continue to cook once out of the oven, so allow for this in calculating the cooking time.

Invert frittata from sauté pan onto serving plate, cut into individual portions and serve warm or at room temperature.

Coppa: The Perfect Accompaniment

Originating from Emilia Romagna, a regional culinary capital of Italy, coppa is made from a whole pork shoulder and fully air-dried to ensure a delicate flavor. When finished, its generous surface reveals red meat flecked with pinkish-white spots of fat. It is cylindrical in shape and should be thinly sliced like prosciutto. Coppa is the perfect accompaniment to mild cheeses, crackers, and red wine.

Fettuccine with Fava Beans and House-Made Ricotta

————•••• ◄─§•●•§─► ••••————

"Let nothing go to waste" is a Volpi philosophy and the spark behind the creation of the Volpini brand of chef-style chopped meats. These nuggets of flavor are an original addition to any pasta, egg, or soup recipe.

§•●•§

Ingredients

1 cup Volpini Prosciutto
4 cups fava beans — fresh and shelled, or frozen
1 pound fettuccine
1½ cups house-made ricotta cheese (*see our recipe on page 86*)
4 oz extra-virgin olive oil
1 Tbsp Italian parsley — fresh, chopped fine
3 tsp lemon zest, freshly grated
sea salt to taste
black pepper to taste, freshly ground

Serves 4–6

§•●•§

Al dente (den' -tay) – Pasta cooked to its proper firmness, known as "to the tooth"

Cooking Method

Place a medium sauté pan over medium heat; add 2 Tbsp olive oil to the pan, along with the Volpini Prosciutto. Cook slowly, allowing the Volpini Prosciutto to render its fat and caramelize. Set aside.

Bring a large pot of well-salted water to a boil. Once at a boil, add pasta and cook until *al dente*, 8 to 10 minutes.

When the fettuccine has 2 to 3 minutes remaining in its cooking, add the fava beans to the pot. (Frozen fava beans can be added directly into the boiling water.) Before straining the fettuccine and fava beans, remove 1½ cups of the pasta water and reserve for sauce.

Strain the fettuccine and fava beans and transfer to large mixing bowl. Drizzle with remaining olive oil, lemon zest, and parsley. Mix well. Incorporate just enough pasta water to provide moisture. Check seasonings, adjust as necessary.

Divide evenly among serving bowls. Place a large dollop of house-made ricotta in the center and garnish with crispy Volpini Prosciutto bits. Serve.

Our History |  | 1930s

The Italian immigrants working at Volpi found their transition to America made easier because their fellow artisans there were very much like them: immigrants from northern Italy who were honoring the old ways and making a new home in a strange land. Italian was the language of choice in the retail store and manufacturing plant, as they practiced their Old World craft with a newfound passion for the opportunities ahead.

Fresh Pappardelle
with Spring Peas and Volpi Prosciutto

The arrival of new produce at the market inspired this recipe. It's simple to create, and it captures the budding flavors of the new season.

Ingredients

1 pound pappardelle pasta (*see our recipe on page 84*)

2 Tbsp extra-virgin olive oil

3 oz Volpi Prosciutto – sliced and julienne-cut

½ cup shallots, julienne-cut

2 tsp garlic – fresh, minced

2 cups spring peas, fresh (frozen can be substituted, if necessary)

½ cup white wine

½ cup vegetable or chicken stock

3 Tbsp butter

1 Tbsp Italian parsley – fresh, chopped

1½ Tbsp basil – fresh, chopped

1 tsp lemon zest, freshly grated

sea salt to taste

black pepper to taste, freshly ground

½ to ¾ cup pecorino cheese, large grate

Serves 4–6

Pisello (pee-zell'-loh) – Garden pea; "pisellini" is the name for baby peas

Cooking Method

Bring a large pot of well-salted water to a boil. Add pasta and cook until *al dente*, 6 to 8 minutes. Remove cooked pasta from water, drain well, and hold warm. Reserve ½ cup of pasta water to finish dish.

Over high heat, add olive oil to a large sauté pan. Once hot, reduce heat to medium-high, add shallots, and cook for 1 minute. Add garlic, cook for one minute, add peas, and cook for another 3 to 4 minutes. Turn heat to high; add white wine, cooking until reduced by half.

Next, add vegetable stock and bring to a boil; add Volpi Prosciutto and cook for one minute. Add ½ cup pasta water and bring to a boil. Add butter and reduce heat to medium-high, until a sauce-like consistency is achieved.

Add pasta, parsley, basil, and lemon zest to sauté pan. Mix well and serve. Garnish with pecorino cheese.

Garden Peas: Summer's First Harvest

A fleeting delight of summer, peas come early in most climates and their delicate flavor is a welcome addition to any meal. Garden or English peas need to be shucked and shouldn't be confused with snap peas or snow peas, both of which have edible pods. The freshest and sweetest peas have supple and shiny green pods. Discerning shoppers can tell if the pods are fresh by taking a handful of pea pods and rubbing them together. If they squeak, they're fresh.

Grilled Prawns Wrapped with
Volpi Pancetta and Herb Vinaigrette

Early spring herbs are a perfect complement to the crispy Volpi Pancetta and deliciously sweet prawns.

Ingredients

Prawns

16 prawns – peeled and deveined
8 slices Volpi Pancetta

Vinaigrette

1 cup extra-virgin olive oil
¼ cup champagne vinegar
1 tsp shallots – fresh, minced
1 Tbsp chervil – fresh, chopped
1 Tbsp chives – fresh, chopped
1 Tbsp Italian parsley – fresh, chopped
2 tsp tarragon – fresh, chopped
2 tsp mint – fresh, chopped
½ tsp lemon zest, freshly grated
sea salt to taste
black pepper to taste, freshly ground

Serves 4

Dragoncello (dra-gahn-chel'-loh) – Tarragon, also goes by l'estragone. First cultivated by the French in 744 A.D.

Cooking Method

Vinaigrette Preparation

Place the vinegar in a medium mixing bowl and slowly whisk in the olive oil to create an emulsion. Once the oil is incorporated, fold in shallots, chervil, chives, parsley, tarragon, mint, and lemon zest. Add salt and pepper to taste. Set aside until prawns are ready to serve.

Prawn Preparation

Take each piece of sliced Volpi Pancetta, unroll and cut in half crosswise to yield 16 pieces. Wrap each of the prawns with the Volpi Pancetta, covering the entire prawn without overlapping.

Heat grill pan to medium-high. Place each of the Volpi Pancetta-wrapped prawns on the grill over medium-high. Cook each side 2 to 3 minutes. The Volpi Pancetta will crisp and the prawns should be just cooked through. Remove to serving dishes. Drizzle herb vinaigrette over the prawns and serve.

Grilling Prawns

The delicately sweet prawn is often confused with shrimp, but the two aren't related, except in their spiny appearance. In fact, the prawn has more in common with a miniature Maine lobster, with its claws and body structure. In summer, prawns can be cooked on the grill, but in the winter prawns can be capably cooked on the stovetop in a sauté pan.

The best method? Place a large sauté pan over medium-high heat, add 1 tablespoon of olive oil, and cook for 2 to 3 minutes. Prawns cook fast, so watch for the skin to turn uniformly pink. Remove and serve.

A walk in a lush garden, the sizzle of meat on the grill, and the dewy freshness of vegetables picked straight from the vine are the hallmarks of this most plentiful of seasons. Mother Nature's abundance is exquisitely on display in these few short months, leaving family gardens awash in herbs, fruits, and vegetables. For the home chef, this bounty makes an admirable pairing with the musky yet delicate essences of prosciutto, salami, and pancetta, each skilled at subtly enhancing even the most simple of flavors. Summer becomes the chef's blank slate, prompting even novices to experiment with its innumerable flavors and tastes.

Summer

Grilled Peaches
with Volpi Prosciutto and Balsamic Glaze

Summertime sparks one of my favorite childhood memories: savoring just-picked peaches from the local farmers market. The size of softballs, they smelled intoxicating and juice covered my chin with the first bite.

Ingredients

2 peaches – ripe, slightly firm

8 thin slices Volpi Prosciutto

3 Tbsp extra-virgin olive oil

1 Tbsp basil – fresh, julienne-cut

1 cup balsamic vinegar

2 oz ricotta salata, thinly shaved

sea salt to taste

black pepper to taste, freshly ground

Serves 4

Griglia (greel'-yah) – Grill; to grill over coals is "alla griglia"

Cooking Method

Place the vinegar in a small non-reactive sauce pot. Place over medium-high heat and bring to a simmer. Reduce heat to low and cook until thick and syrup-like. Remove from heat; cool.

Cut each peach in half and remove pit. Lightly coat each peach half with olive oil. Season with salt and pepper.

Place the peaches flesh-side down over medium-hot charcoals. If using the outdoor grill is not an option or time is an issue, a hot-stove griddle pan will do the trick. Cook for 2 to 3 minutes. Once golden brown, turn over and cook the skin-side for another minute. Remove from grill and set aside.

Place two slices of Volpi Prosciutto on each serving plate. Place a grilled peach next to the Volpi Prosciutto. Liberally drizzle the balsamic reduction over each peach, followed by a light drizzle of your favorite olive oil. Sprinkle basil over top and garnish with ricotta salata.

Prosciutto Crudo: The Quintessential Dry-Cured Meat

For more than 2,000 years, Italians have used three ingredients to produce this savory and delicate meat: whole, bone-in ham legs, sea salt, and time. The process begins with superior quality ham followed by sea-salt massages and leisurely stays in curing rooms to wick the water from the meat. The subtle and sweet flavors of prosciutto come from its lengthy aging process, taking as long as 36 months in some cases. Prosciutto's silky texture complements its musky scent and velvety taste.

Spinach Risotto
with Marscapone and Volpi Bresaola

Time, patience, and thought go into the preparation of risotto. Fresh spinach, with its lively color and wonderful flavor, is an ideal partner for this Italian staple.

Ingredients

4 cups chicken stock

2 Tbsp extra-virgin olive oil

1 onion, medium – small dice

1 tsp garlic – fresh, minced

2 cups Arborio rice

½ cup white wine

1 pound spinach, fresh

1 Tbsp Italian parsley, finely chopped

¼ cup parmesan cheese

2 Tbsp butter, unsalted

2 tsp lemon zest, freshly grated

sea salt to taste

black pepper to taste, freshly ground

2 Tbsp mascarpone cheese

6 oz Volpi Bresaola, julienne-cut

Serves 4–6

Saporito (sa-po-ree' -toh) – Flavorful

Cooking Method

Bring 4 quarts of water to a boil; add 2 Tbsp of salt. Prepare a large bowl as ice bath to shock spinach and stop cooking process. Place the spinach, in batches, into boiling water for 30 seconds. Remove and "shock" in ice bath. Once cool, remove and squeeze with your hands to remove excess water. Rough-chop spinach, then place in bowl of food processor. Pulse machine to create a smooth puree. If necessary, add a small amount of the blanching water to obtain the proper consistency. Reserve 1 cup of the blanch water for risotto.

Place chicken stock and the reserved blanch water in a sauce pot and warm.

In a large heavy-bottom sauce pot, heat olive oil over medium heat. Add onions, garlic, and a pinch of salt. Sauté until the onions are soft and translucent, 5 to 6 minutes. Add rice and, constantly stirring, sauté for a few minutes. Rice will take on a "pearled" or shiny appearance. Add wine and simmer until fully absorbed.

Add chicken stock to just cover the rice. Increase heat to medium-high; stir continuously. Add stock one ladle at a time as the rice absorbs it. Cook 15 to 20 minutes; the rice will take on a creamy texture. Once the rice is *al dente*, add the spinach purée and stir quickly. Remove from heat; add butter, lemon zest, and parmesan cheese.

Divide equally among serving dishes; garnish with mascarpone and Volpi Bresaola.

Bresaola: Bringing Beef to the Fore

Salted and dried tenderloin or beef fillet, bresaola is the leanest of the Italian cured meats. Bresaola is massaged with salt and seasonings, which vary according to tradition but include juniper berries, bay leaf, or clove. Its burgundy-red color has little visible fat, giving the moist and delicate slices a rich feel and taste. A delicacy rubbed with spices and naturally air-cured, bresaola can be served as thin slices around Parmigiano-Reggiano cheese or prepared as ruffles for a simple but elegant hors d'oeuvre.

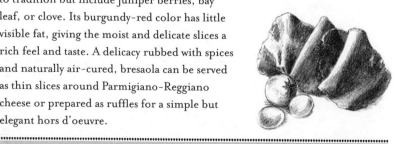

Stuffed Baked Cherry Tomatoes

A morning walk to the garden inspired this dish. As we all know, one tomato plant offers a bounty of fruit, so I developed the perfect snack for any time of the day.

Ingredients

20 large cherry tomatoes
2 Tbsp breadcrumbs
sea salt to taste
black pepper to taste, freshly ground

Fillings

1 oz zucchini — small, cubed into 4 pieces
1 oz mozzarella — fresh, diced into 4 pieces
½ oz green olives, minced
½ oz kalamata olives, minced
1 oz artichoke hearts, chopped
1 oz tuna, drained, divided into 4 chunks
3 oz Volpi Prosciutto, small dice
3 Tbsp extra-virgin olive oil
2 tsp garden herbs: fresh basil, Italian parsley, chives — chopped
1 oz parmesan cheese, grated

Serves 4

Spuntino (spun–tee´–noh) – Snack

Cooking Method

Preheat oven to 350° F. Place small sauté pan over medium heat; add olive oil and Volpi Prosciutto. Cook slowly to render fat and caramelize to a golden brown. Remove from heat and set aside.

Trim approx. $^1/_8$-inch from the top of each tomato; place tops in a 9-inch baking dish. Season tomato tops with salt and pepper. Using a small spoon, remove the seeds from the tomatoes.

Stuffing Method - 4 each per flavor profile

Season zucchini cubes with salt and pepper; place 1 cube per tomato. Place in baking dish.

Place mozzarella cubes inside 4 more tomatoes; place in baking dish.

Mix green and kalamata olives together; fill 4 more tomatoes and place in baking dish.

Season artichoke hearts with salt and pepper; fill 4 more tomatoes and place in baking dish.

Lightly season the tuna with salt and pepper; fill 4 more tomatoes and place in baking dish.

In a small bowl, combine bread crumbs and fresh herbs. Season with salt and pepper and top each tomato with mixture. Drizzle olive oil over each of the tomatoes and their tops. Sprinkle each tomato, with the exception of tuna, with parmesan cheese. Bake for 10 to 12 minutes until warm. Remove and garnish with toasted Volpi Prosciutto bits.

Oven-Roasted Chicken Breast with Corn, Green Beans, and Volpi Pancetta Ragu

Summer's hallmark, the voluptuous corn on the cob makes a dramatic addition to this spectacular dish.

Ingredients

4 chicken breasts – bone-in, skin on
2 cups corn on cob, approx. 3 ears
I cup green beans – fresh, cut into thirds
2¼ Tbsp extra-virgin olive oil
4 oz Volpi Pancetta – cut to ¼-inch lardons
2 Tbsp champagne vinegar
4 oz chicken stock
2 Tbsp butter, unsalted
2 tsp oregano – fresh, chopped
sea salt to taste
black pepper to taste, freshly ground

Serves 4

Fagiolino (fa-jio-lee'-no) – Beans, and green beans are known as "fagiolini"

Cooking Method

Preheat oven to 450° F. Bring a large stock pot of water to boil; add salt. Place corn in pot and cook for 2 to 3 minutes until tender. Remove and set aside to cool. Drop green beans into boiling water and cook until tender, 3 to 4 minutes. Remove from pot; cool. Once cooled, shave kernels off the cob and place in medium mixing bowl and add green beans. Set aside.

Place 1 tsp olive oil in small sauté pan over medium heat. Place Volpi Pancetta in pan and allow to render slowly until crisp and golden brown, 6 to 8 minutes. Remove from pan to paper towel. Reserve fat for sautéing chicken breasts.

Season chicken breasts with salt and pepper. Place a large sauté pan over medium-high heat; add reserved Volpi Pancetta fat and 1 Tbsp olive oil. When pan is hot, place chicken skin-side down to cook. Allow skin to crisp before turning, 3 to 5 minutes. Turn chicken breast over and place in oven to finish cooking, 15 to 20 minutes. Remove chicken breasts from oven and set aside.

Place the pan over medium-high heat; add 1 Tbsp olive oil. Once pan is hot, add the corn and green bean mixture; season with salt and pepper. Cook quickly to warm, 1 minute. Add chicken stock and bring to a simmer. Finish with butter, Volpi Pancetta, and oregano. Remove from heat, add champagne vinegar, and toss. Adjust seasoning as necessary.

Divide ragu evenly between plates; include equal amounts of pan *jus*. Place chicken breast on top of ragu and serve.

Lardons

A French term, "lardon" generally refers to bacon that has been diced and then fried or blanched. The thinly sliced pieces of fatback and salt pork are used to add flavor by inserting them raw into lean meats (the so-called process of larding) or adding them fried to salads, stews, and egg dishes. For best results, fry the lardons over medium heat to render the fat and turn them a crispy brown. With their distinctive rich and salty flavor, lardons are often used as a great base for browning vegetables and meat.

Linguine with Volpi Calabrese Salami, Peppers, Onions, Mushrooms, and Arugula

This combination of ingredients delivers on all levels: spicy, sweet, earthy, and aromatic. This is one of those recipes you'll soon feel you can't live without.

Ingredients

1 pound linguine pasta, dried
1 pound sweet Italian sausage
1 pound Volpi Calabrese Salami, small dice
3 red bell peppers, julienne-cut
2 sweet onions, julienne-cut
½ pound crimini mushrooms, sliced
2 Tbsp garlic – fresh, sliced
½ cup basil – fresh, julienne-cut
3 Tbsp butter
4 Tbsp extra-virgin olive oil
sea salt to taste
black pepper to taste, freshly ground
1 cup parmesan cheese, grated

Serves 6

Cipolla (chee-poll'-lah) – Onion

Cooking Method

Heat 1 Tbsp olive oil in large sauté pan until hot. Add sausage in nickel-size pieces. Without stirring, cook for 3 to 4 minutes to caramelize. Add the diced Volpi Calabrese Salami and sauté until cooked through, 3 to 4 minutes. Remove and set aside.

Bring a large pot of well-salted water to a boil. Add pasta and cook until *al dente*, 9 to 11 minutes. Reserve 2 cups of pasta water for pan sauce.

Add 2 Tbsp olive oil to large sauté pan and heat until hot. Add sliced mushrooms; toss and spread over bottom of pan. Do not stir. Season with salt and pepper. Allow mushrooms to turn golden brown, 5 to 7 minutes cooking time; toss again. Remove and set aside.

Add 1 Tbsp olive oil to large sauté pan, heat until hot. Add bell peppers and onions. Toss and spread over the bottom of the pan. Do not stir. Season with salt and pepper, cooking until onions caramelize, 6 to 8 minutes. Add sliced garlic. Cook until garlic is golden brown.

Add sausage, Volpi Calabrese Salami, and mushroom mixture back to the pan. Mix well. Add reserved pasta water and bring to a boil. Reduce by half, add butter, and remove from heat.

Place pasta in a large, warmed mixing bowl. Add sausage mixture and fresh basil. Mix well. Spoon the pasta and sausage mixture onto each plate. Garnish with grated parmesan.

Salami and Your Health

Moderation is the watchword in good Italian cooking and eating. With such fine products, it would be wasteful to pile up large quantities of meat and miss the delicate essence of prosciutto or the vital spirit of salami. Shave paper-thin slices for antipasto and sandwiches to ensure the flavors burst forth and calories are kept in check. Volpi uses high-quality meat, and the curing process strips much of the fat (mostly unsaturated) and cholesterol from its meat products. Salame, which is high in B vitamins, is also packed with important minerals, including iron, zinc, chromium, selenium, and magnesium.

Volpi Deli Antipasto Salad

Antipasto fits just about any occasion because it's packed with flavor and variety. Not even picky eaters can resist the wealth of distinctive tastes found in this cornucopia of ingredients.

Ingredients

1 pound penne or fusilli pasta
8 oz Volpi Genova salami, small dice
4 oz Volpi Pepperoni, small dice
¾ oz pepperocini, sliced into rings
8 oz ceci (garbanzo beans), drained
1 oz red onion, thin julienne-cut
3 oz kalamata olives, quartered
3 oz green olives, quartered
5 oz roasted bell peppers, small dice
6 oz smoked mozzarella, small dice
2 Tbsp Italian parsley – fresh, chopped
2 Tbsp basil – fresh, chopped
½ cup parmesan, grated
1 pint sweet cherry tomatoes, cut in half

Marinade

1 Tbsp garlic, minced and toasted
2 cups extra-virgin olive oil
²/₃ cup red wine vinegar
sea salt to taste
black pepper to taste, freshly ground

Serves 6–8

Cece (chee'-chee) – Garbanzo bean or chickpea

Cooking Method

Bring a large pot of well-salted water to a boil. Add pasta and cook until *al dente*, 10 to 12 minutes. While the pasta is cooking, assemble the salad dressing.

A large mixing bowl is required for this recipe; you'll need plenty of room to get all the ingredients mixed together well. As each of the ingredients is prepped, place into the large bowl. Reserve the parsley, basil, and parmesan cheese for last step.

Place garlic in a small sauté pan over medium heat and cook until golden brown. Place vinegar in a blender. Using high speed, slowly pour in the olive oil. Once the oil is incorporated, add garlic, salt, and pepper to taste.

Slice the cherry tomatoes in half; season with salt and pepper and drizzle with olive oil. Set aside.

Finish the antipasto salad by draining the pasta and placing in a large bowl. (You'll need plenty of room to get all the ingredients mixed together.) Add your antipasto dressing to the pasta while it is still warm. As the pasta cools, it absorbs the dressing, capturing all the flavors. Mix well. Add parsley, basil, and parmesan to finish. Garnish with cherry tomatoes.

Volpi History |  | 1940s

When America went to war in 1941, even the steadiest business hands were challenged by the resulting shortages, especially the scarcity of meat. Many dry-cured meats companies around the country were unable to keep their doors open during this difficult period, but John Volpi and Company shouldered on, continuing to produce its fine quality dry-cured meats.

Volpi Pancetta-Wrapped Salmon with Vine-Ripe Tomato and Corn Salsa

As ripe summer tomatoes fall from the vine and the corn weighs down the stalks, this recipe is the perfect antidote for a garden bursting with produce, begging to be picked.

Ingredients

8 slices Volpi Pancetta
4 salmon fillets – 6 oz each, skin removed
2 Tbsp extra-virgin olive oil
sea salt to taste
black pepper to taste, freshly ground

Salsa

2 cups corn on cob, approx. 3 ears
4 vine-ripe tomatoes, ½-inch dice
¼ cup red onion, minced
1 Tbsp Italian parsley – fresh, chopped
1 Tbsp basil – fresh, julienne-cut
1 Tbsp lemon juice, fresh
2 Tbsp extra-virgin olive oil
sea salt to taste
black pepper to taste, freshly ground

Serves 4

Granoturco (gran-oh-tur´-koh) – Corn

Cooking Method

Bring a large stock pot of water to a boil; add sea salt. Place corn in pot and cook for 2 to 3 minutes until tender. Remove and set aside. Once corn has cooled, shave the kernels off the cob and place in medium mixing bowl.

Add tomatoes, red onion, parsley, basil, lemon juice, and olive oil to the corn. Mix well. Season with salt and pepper and set aside.

Preheat oven to 450° F. Use two pieces of Volpi Pancetta per salmon fillet. Lightly season each fillet with salt and pepper. Gently wrap each piece of salmon; cover the fillets completely but do not overlap.

Place olive oil in large sauté pan over medium-high heat, presentation-side down first. Allow to cook untouched for 3 to 4 minutes until golden brown. Turn fillet over, remove pan from stove, and place in oven. Cook for another 3 to 4 minutes or to individual taste.

Remove from oven and set aside. Check the seasoning of salsa; adjust as necessary. Divide the salsa evenly between serving plates. Place a salmon fillet atop the mixture and drizzle your favorite olive oil to finish.

Chef's note: Look for salmon fillets that are similar in size and thickness. This will ensure even cooking time and a proper degree of temperature for each fillet.

The Versatile Pancetta

Salt-cured and spiced, pancetta is a rich and marbled pork belly, tightly rolled to keep in its delicate flavors. This is the same cut used to make bacon, although pancetta is cured with salt, spices, and herbs and then air-dried. Its savory taste lends itself to pasta dishes, pizza, or as an accompaniment to other meat dishes. Often pan-fried to a crisp, pancetta is then crumbled and added to dishes or wrapped around pieces of meat and fish.

Volpi Bresaola Carpaccio with Shaved Fennel and Celery Hearts Salad

Antipasto, meaning "before the meal," is the traditional introductory course for formal Italian meals, and each region claims its own special components.

Ingredients

12 thin slices Volpi Bresaola
½ cup fennel bulb, thinly shaved
¼ cup celery hearts, thinly shaved
¼ pound Parmigiano-Reggiano
2 oz extra-virgin olive oil
1 Tbsp lemon juice, fresh
sea salt to taste
black pepper to taste, freshly ground

Serves 4

Finocchio (fee-nock'-kee-oh) – Fennel, stems, leaves, seeds, and roots used for cooking

Cooking Method

Arrange the Volpi Bresaola on a large serving platter, drizzle with ½ oz olive oil.

In a medium bowl, combine the fennel and celery hearts. Drizzle remaining olive oil and lemon juice over top. Lightly season with salt and pepper; mix well.

Scatter this mixture over the platter of Volpi Bresaola. Garnish with large ribbons of Parmigiano-Reggiano.

An Old World Classic: Parmigiano-Reggiano

A celebrity in the cheese world, Parmigiano-Reggiano has an intense, rich flavor that is moist when young and grainier as it ages. Produced in particular northern regions of Italy, it is distinguished from other cheeses by the Italian government. Each individual producer maintains a consistent savory quality, with slight flavor variations by region. A wheel weighs in at some 60 pounds (30 kilograms), and experienced chefs often save the rinds to flavor stews, stocks, or sauces.

Volpi Italian "Hero"

One of the great joys in life is the perfect sandwich, and one of the best is loaded with a variety of Volpi-cured Italian meats.

Ingredients

1 Italian baguette or ciabatta, freshly baked
8 slices Volpi Prosciutto
8 slices Volpi Capocolla
8 slices Volpi Coppa
8 slices Volpi Genova Salami
6 slices Volpi Mortadella
8 slices Volpi Milano Salami
8 slices Volpi Sopressata
6 slices provolone
1½ oz pepperocini, sliced
4 oz roasted bell peppers
½ medium red onion, sliced thin
1½ cup arugula
extra-virgin olive oil to taste
red wine vinegar to taste
sea salt to taste
black pepper to taste, freshly ground
4 to 6 skewers

Serves 4–6

Aceto di vino (ah-chay'-toh dee vee'-noh) – Wine vinegar

Cooking Method

Split the Italian baguette in half lengthwise, leaving the back edge attached. Open fully and flatten. Drizzle with olive oil and red wine vinegar; season with salt and pepper.

Layer the meats so that they overlap slightly as you build the sandwich. Make sure the entire length of the baguette is covered.

Next, layer the provolone, followed by the pepperocini, roasted bell peppers, and red onion slices.

Place the arugula in a small mixing bowl. Lightly dress with olive oil and vinegar, salt and pepper to taste. Mix well. Distribute evenly over the length of the baguette.

Fold the baguette to form sandwich, and place skewers an even distance apart to hold together. Cut into individual sandwiches.

Our Hero Sandwich

Italian Americans living on the East Coast originated these large sandwiches known as much for their size as their many monikers: grinder, submarine, hoagie, poor boy, and hero, to name a few. Geography determined the name and many of the ingredients (everything from hot peppers to lettuce and tomatoes). At the heart of the sandwich, though, is a deli counter full of sliced meats. They say the hero, which was popular with Italian laborers in New York in the late nineteenth century, first got its name in the 1930s when a food writer said you needed to be a "hero" to finish one of these enormous Italian sandwiches.

Volpi Pancetta, Lettuce, and Tomato Panini

A twist to the iconic American favorite, the "BLT," this is one of my fondest memories of my days spent as a chef at the restaurant Tra Vigne.

Ingredients

8 oz Volpi Pancetta, sliced
8 slices pugliese or hard-crusted bread, lightly toasted
3 large vine-ripened tomatoes, sliced
2 cups mixed greens
½ cup mayonnaise

Serves 4

Pomodoro (poh–moh–doh'–roh) – Tomato

Cooking Method

Preheat oven to 375° F. Cook the Volpi Pancetta on a parchment-lined sheet pan and cook until crisp and golden brown. Remove from oven and place on paper towel to drain.

While the Volpi Pancetta is cooking, lightly toast the pugliese. Once cooled, liberally coat each piece with mayonnaise.

Evenly distribute the cooked Volpi Pancetta atop half of the bread, followed by handful of mixed greens and sliced tomatoes. Season with salt and pepper. Top each with the remaining slices of bread and press firmly. Cut in half on the bias and serve.

Chef's note: Take this sandwich to the next level by adding freshly chopped basil (1 Tbsp) to the mayonnaise before building the sandwich.

Tomato: A Fruit with a Past

The plump and juicy tomato is inextricably linked to Italian cooking today, but that hasn't always been true. Once considered poisonous, the tomato was only an ornamental element in homes for many years, and it wasn't used for food until a famine prompted locals to eat their decorative art. Soon, the tomato was a staple of the Italian diet. It is best to eat them fresh when in season, or canned out of season. Fresh tomatoes should not be stored in the refrigerator, although sliced ones should be refrigerated. A ripe tomato will last several days on the countertop.

As autumn takes hold, and our days slip deeper into darkness, the change of seasons brings a glorious harvest—at once rustic and welcoming. Squash and root vegetables flourish as summer recedes, bringing the distinct taste of well-tended soil and the crispness of autumn. Fall fruits are in season, with persimmons, pears, pomegranates, and apples overflowing with their brawny sweetness. The delicate ripeness of proscuitto, bresaola, and pancetta is swathed by these earthy flavors, serving in this season to merely complement not conquer them, while heartier meats like coppa, sopressata, and pepperoni match these savory delights in pungency and flavor.

Autumn

Oven-Roasted Acorn Squash
with Crispy Volpi Pancetta

The simplicity of preparation and ease of cooking make this an ideal dish for brisk autumn nights.

Ingredients

2 medium acorn squash

4 oz Volpi Pancetta, ¼-inch square lardons

1 tsp extra-virgin olive oil

1 stick butter, unsalted

1 Tbsp sage — fresh, chopped fine

½ cup brown sugar

2 oz molasses

sea salt to taste

black pepper to taste, freshly ground

Serves 4

Zucca (tsook´-kah) — Winter squash or pumpkin

Cooking Method

Preheat oven to 375° F. Using a sharp knife on a firm surface, cut the squash in half, horizontally, then cut a thin sliver of skin from the back side of the squash to provide stability while cooking. Scrape out the seeds and discard.

Place the squash halves on a sheet pan lined with aluminum foil. Season with salt and pepper; set aside.

Heat olive oil in a large sauté pan over medium-high heat. Add Volpi Pancetta and allow it to render until crisp and golden brown. Remove from pan.

Add butter to sauté pan and cook until it has browned. Immediately remove from heat. Add sage, brown sugar, and molasses. Place sauté pan back over low heat and cook until brown sugar has melted and all ingredients are well-combined. Distribute the mixture evenly between the 4 halves of squash. Place in oven and roast until the flesh is tender, approx. 1 hour. At 15-minute intervals, baste the top flesh of the squash with the liquid that has collected in the center cavity. In the last 5 minutes of cooking, sprinkle the Volpi Pancetta lardons over each serving of squash.

Why Dry Curing?

For John Volpi and Company, the chosen method for preserving fine meat is through dry curing—a combination of salt curing and air-drying. Commonly, dry-cured meats are swathed in salt and then air-dried for various time periods, depending on the meat product. The key to the dry-curing process is the salt. Volpi uses the finest quality sea salt to reduce the moisture content in the meat and to make a hostile environment for bacteria. During the curing process, meat products can lose up to 50 percent of their weight as the salt wicks the moisture from the meat.

Polenta with Wild Mushroom Bolognese

Polenta is truly one of those "feel good" dishes, and its creamy texture contrasts here with fall's rustic mushrooms.

Ingredients

¼ pound chanterelle mushrooms, medium dice
¼ pound crimini mushrooms, medium dice
¼ pound shiitake mushrooms, medium dice
4 Tbsp extra-virgin olive oil
½ cup onion, small dice
½ cup carrot, small dice
¼ cup fennel, small dice
¼ pound pork, ground
¼ pound veal, ground
¼ pound beef, ground
¼ pound Volpi Pancetta, small dice
2 cups chicken stock
1 Tbsp flour
2 Tbsp butter, unsalted
½ cup Italian parsley — fresh, chopped
2 Tbsp parmesan cheese, grated
5 cups polenta

For our Creamy Polenta recipe, see the Everyday Dishes section on page 87.

Serves 4

Brodo (broh´-do) – Broth or stock from boiled meats or vegetables

Cooking Method

Place 3 Tbsp of olive oil in a large sauté pan over high heat. Once oil is hot, add the mushrooms and let sit. Cook for a few minutes, season with salt and pepper, and toss. Continue cooking until mushrooms are caramelized and golden brown, 5 to 7 minutes. Remove from pan; keep warm.

In the same sauté pan add 1 Tbsp olive oil and place over high heat. Once hot, add pork, veal, beef, and Volpi Pancetta. Season with salt and pepper and cook for 5 minutes, stirring occasionally. Add onions, carrots, and fennel. Season with salt and pepper. Cook an additional 5 to 7 minutes or until the vegetables are just tender. Add cooked mushrooms back to pan.

Sprinkle the flour on top and mix well. Add chicken stock and bring to a boil, then reduce to a simmer and cook until sauce consistency is achieved. Check and adjust seasoning as necessary. Remove from heat; stir in butter and parsley.

Prepare polenta per the recommended directions. Place hot polenta in serving bowl. Top with wild mushroom ragu and garnish with parmesan cheese. Serve immediately.

The Ubiquitous Parsley

Italian parsley (*prezzemolo*) is flat-leafed and sweeter than the standard curly-leaf variety, which is often used as decoration on restaurant dinner plates. With more essential oils than its cousin, Italian parsley brightens dishes and soups, and it is easier to chop with its wide, flat leaves. Parsley is such a favorite of chefs everywhere that it's a universal sidekick in cooking and a popular plant in kitchen and windowsill gardens. In fact, the ever-present parsley serves as a social metaphor in Italy: a frequent party guest is drolly described as *il prezzemolo*, as "being like parsley."

Volpi Bresaola and Volpi Coppa with Shaved Fennel, Cucumber, and Smoked Almonds Salad

This is a dish that can be prepared on individual plates or on a platter to serve family-style. I let the theme of the party or the meal guide its best presentation.

Ingredients

6 oz Volpi Bresaola, sliced thin
6 oz Volpi Coppa, sliced thin
1 fennel bulb, medium – reserve 2 Tbsp frawns for garnish
1 cucumber – peeled, remove seeds
$^1/_3$ cup smoked almonds
3 oz parmesan cheese
2 oz extra-virgin olive oil, new-press preferred (*see olive oil facts on page 49*)
sea salt to taste

Serves 6

Mandorla (mahn'-dor-lah) – Almond

Cooking Method

Place equal amounts of Volpi Bresaola and Volpi Coppa on each serving plate, slightly overlapping and alternating meats as each is assembled.

Cut thin slices of cucumber on the bias to create crescent shaped pieces. Trim the fennel bulb and thinly shave it to create julienne pieces.

Combine cucumber and fennel in medium mixing bowl, lightly season with salt, and mix well. Place a small mound of this mixture in the center of each plate.

Slice or roughly chop the smoked almonds and sprinkle on top. Add a light drizzle of olive oil over the meats and salad.

Using a vegetable peeler, create 3 or 4 ribbons of parmesan for each plate. Finish the dish with the fennel frawns.

Fresh Off the Presses: Olive Oil

While there are thousands of olive types or cultivars, only a small number are grown for olive oil. Oil processing begins with washing the fruit, followed by crushing, decanting or pressing, separation, and filtration. Extra-virgin olive oil (EVOO) has superior taste and exceptionally low acidity (below 0.8 percent), while virgin olive oil has good flavor and acidity below 2 percent. Superior oils are fruity (reflecting its cultivar); bitter (prompted by unripe or green olives); and pungent (the pungent taste resulting from production). Real aficionados love new-press olive oil, which is intense and superbly flavorful—a rare treat for dipping and cooking.

Oven–Roasted Brussel Sprouts with Volpi Pancetta

This recipe truly captures the heartier flavors of the autumn season. It is my favorite time of year because it is filled with so many Laukert family celebrations.

Ingredients

1½ pounds brussel sprouts

6 oz Volpi Pancetta, cut in ⅛-inch square lardons

½ onion, medium, small dice

1 tsp garlic – fresh, chopped

1 Tbsp extra-virgin olive oil

½ cup chicken stock

1 Tbsp butter

sea salt to taste

black pepper to taste, freshly ground

1 Tbsp lemon juice (optional)

Serves 6

Maiale (mah–ee–ah' –lay) – Pork

Cooking Method

Preheat oven to 400° F. Trim the ends of the brussel sprouts and make an "x" in the core to ensure thorough cooking.

Bring a large pot of salted water to a boil. Drop in brussel sprouts and blanch for 3 minutes. Remove, drain well, and allow to cool. Cut sprouts in half.

Place olive oil in a large heavy-gauge pan over medium heat. Add Volpi Pancetta lardons and render until golden brown and crisp, approx. 3 minutes. Remove and set aside.

Add onions to pan and cook until translucent, 3 to 4 minutes. Add garlic and continue cooking a few more minutes.

Add brussel sprouts and Volpi Pancetta back to the pan; season with salt and pepper. Mix well and place in oven. Roast for additional 5 to 7 minutes until golden brown and tender.

To finish, place pan on high heat, add chicken stock, and reduce by half. Remove from heat and add butter. Check seasoning. If using the lemon juice, add as a finish to the dish.

Chef's note: This is the perfect recipe for you to use a cast-iron pan. The even heat and ability to maintain an even temperature will ensure perfect roasting of your sprouts.

Volpi History | **VOLPI** THE TASTE OF ITALY SINCE 1902 | Early 1950s

With the war over and rationing ended, John Volpi and Company prospered and continued to expand production. Word spread of Volpi's superior quality, and soon Volpi products were finding their way to new markets in Chicago and New York. The company embraced government efforts to regulate the production of the dry-cured meats to ensure the highest-quality product for customers, as many families began to include dry-cured meat products in their kitchens and pantries.

Grilled Radicchio
with Volpi Prosciutto Vinaigrette

Grilling mellows the flavor and incorporates a wonderful smokiness in this slightly bitter and spicy vegetable. It's versatile enough to be a side vegetable or an addition to salads, risottos, and pastas.

Ingredients

2 heads radicchio — medium-size, trimmed, cut into quarters

3 oz Volpi Prosciutto — sliced, cut into ¼-inch julienne strips

1 cup extra-virgin olive oil

¼ cup balsamic vinegar

2 Tbsp butter, unsalted

1 tsp thyme — fresh, chopped

1 Tbsp Dijon mustard

¼ cup water

sea salt to taste

black pepper to taste, freshly ground

Serves 6–8

Olio d'oliva (oh'-lee-oh doh-lee'-vah) — Pure olive oil coming from native and refined oil

Cooking Method

Place cut quarters of radicchio in bowl of ice water to soak for 15 minutes. Remove and pat dry before grilling.

Place 2 Tbsp of butter in a medium sauté pan over medium-low heat. Place Volpi Prosciutto in sauté pan, allowing it to slowly render. Once crisp and golden brown, remove from pan. Into the hot pan, add thyme. Remove from heat and set aside.

In a blender add vinegar and mustard. On medium speed, slowly add ¾ cup olive oil. As the vinaigrette thickens, adjust consistency with water. Transfer all of the thyme, Volpi Prosciutto fat, and butter from the sauté pan into the blender. Add salt, pepper, and lemon zest. Pulse quickly just to incorporate. Check seasonings, set aside.

Preheat grill or grill pan to medium-high heat. Lightly brush the radicchio with olive oil; season with salt and pepper. Grill for 2 to 3 minutes. Turn radicchio to other cut side and cook additional 2 to 3 minutes. Once tender and showing nice char from grilling, remove to serving platter. Drizzle vinaigrette over each of the wedges and garnish with crispy Volpi Prosciutto.

Sonda: The Horse-Bone Needle

A prosciutto master has many tools but none more important than the sonda, a pointed needle carved from the shinbone of a horse. Throughout the curing process, the master periodically probes the inside muscle of the ham with a sonda to test its maturity. It's not only a traditional tool used by Old World prosciutto masters; it is the most effective method for determining if a ham has spoiled. The porous bone quickly picks up the scent of the interior of the ham, and if it is pleasingly maturing, the needle will smell sweet when it's removed.

Linguine with Clam Sauce and Volpi Calabrese Salami

As a young cook, this was one of the first pasta dishes I mastered—an Americanized interpretation, of course. As I matured as a chef, I added my own flavor nuances to this classic Italian dish.

Ingredients

I pound linguine pasta, dried
2 pounds little neck clams, cleaned
8 oz Volpi Calabrese Salami, small dice
¼ cup extra-virgin olive oil
3 Tbsp garlic – fresh, thinly sliced
¼ tsp crushed red chili flakes
I cup white wine
½ cup clam juice
I Tbsp lemon juice, fresh
¼ cup Italian parsley – fresh, chopped
2 Tbsp butter, unsalted
sea salt to taste
black pepper to taste, freshly ground

Serves 4–6

Alla diavolo (dee-ah´-voh-loh) – Devil's style or spicy

Cooking Method

Bring a large pot of well-salted water to a boil over high heat. Add linguine and cook per the recommended directions, usually 8 to 10 minutes or until pasta is *al dente*. Drain well and set aside. Reserve 2 cups of the pasta cooking liquid for the sauce.

Place a large sauté pan (with a cover) over medium-high heat; add olive oil. Once oil is hot add the Volpi Calabrese Salami and cook until slightly caramelized, 2 to 3 minutes. Add the sliced garlic. Add chili flakes once the garlic turns golden brown. Add clam juice and white wine to deglaze sauté pan, then include the clams and cover immediately. Cook for 5 to 7 minutes, shaking the sauté pan occasionally to make clams open.

Remove cover. Discard clams that have not opened. Finish the sauce with lemon juice, butter, and parsley. Check seasoning; adjust as necessary.

Add pasta to pan and mix well. Divide evenly between serving bowls.

Volpi History | **VOLPI** THE TASTE OF ITALY SINCE 1902 | Late 1950s

Sadness filled the business with the deaths of John Volpi and Gino Pasetti. The master artisans passed their business to their enterprising nephew, the well-trained Armando, certain that the Volpi history of superior service and high quality would continue. After nearly 20 years in the business, Armando was poised to carry on his uncles' work and continue the traditions that had long distinguished Volpi from its many competitors.

Pork Loin Saltimbocca with Volpi Pancetta and Sweet Potato Mashers

Volpi Pancetta comes elegantly sliced for just these occasions, making it easy for amateur and experienced cooks to pull off a classic dish like this one.

Ingredients

1½ pounds pork loin, sliced

8 ea Volpi Pancetta, sliced thin

16 sage leaves

3 Tbsp extra-virgin olive oil

1 Tbsp butter, unsalted

¼ cup white wine

¼ cup chicken stock

1½ cups flour, for dredging pork

sea salt to taste

black pepper to taste, freshly ground

8 toothpicks

Visit the Volpi website (volpifoods.com) for our Sweet Potato Mashers recipe.

Serves 4

Salvia (sahl'-vee-ah) – Sage, usually used to accompany roasted dishes

Cooking Method

Preheat oven to 350° F. Place cutlets on cutting board, allowing extra space between each cutlet. Gently pound the meat until ¼-inch thick.

Place 2 sage leaves on each pork cutlet, then top with Volpi Pancetta. Secure with a toothpick. Lightly dredge the pork cutlet in well-seasoned flour; shake well to remove excess flour.

Place 1½ Tbsp olive oil in a large sauté pan over medium-high heat. Once hot, add the meat in small batches, Volpi Pancetta-side down first. Cook for 2 to 3 minutes, allowing the Volpi Pancetta to become crisp and golden brown. Turn; cook for additional 2 to 3 minutes or until it's done to your specifications. Remove toothpicks and place on holding plate. Continue process until all of the cutlets have been cooked.

Deglaze the sauté pan with white wine. Add chicken stock and bring to a simmer. Check seasoning; adjust as necessary. Remove from heat, add butter, and whisk. Keep warm.

Place two each of the pork loin saltimbocca on each plate and spoon a small amount of the pan *jus* over each pork cutlet. Add a large scoop of sweet potato mashers to each plate and serve.

A Sweet Potato by any Other Name

A native plant to America that's firmly rooted in the Italian cooking lexicon, the sweet potato comes in two varieties in the United States. Southern cooks prefer the orange, sweet, and moist-flesh variety, while northerners have taken to the yellow, mealy, and dry-flesh version. Sweet potatoes are called yams in the U.S., but true yams are found mainly in Africa and weigh as much as 100 pounds apiece. A nutritional jackpot, sweet potatoes are high in protein, fiber, vitamin C, calcium, folic acid, and magnesium.

Bruschetta: Volpi Prosciutto and Fig & Volpi Bresaola and Honeycomb

I really prefer to utilize a stovetop grill pan for these two bruschetta variations because of the smoky flavor that infuses the bread during grilling.

Ingredients

8 slices pugliese bread, ½-inch thick

4 slices Volpi Prosciutto

8 slices Volpi Bresaola

12 figs — fresh, sliced in half

8 tsp honeycomb, ½-inch cubes — orange blossom recommended

2 oz pecorino cheese

2 oz ricotta salata

I tsp orange zest, freshly grated

extra-virgin olive oil, new-press preferred (*see olive oil facts on page 49*)

sea salt to taste

black pepper to taste, freshly ground

Serves 4

Miele (mee-ay'-lay) – Honey

Cooking Method

Place grill pan over medium-high heat. Once hot, grill each side of the bruschetta until golden brown and soft inside, with a crisp outer crust. Remove to sheet pan. Apply a very light drizzle of olive oil and season with salt and pepper.

Bruschetta with Volpi Prosciutto and Figs

Take 4 toasted bruschetta; place a full slice of Volpi Prosciutto on top. Move to serving dish. Place the cut figs around the platter; add another light drizzle of olive oil. Using a vegetable peeler, create ribbons of pecorino cheese over the bruschetta.

Bruschetta with Volpi Bresaola and Honeycomb

Take 4 toasted bruschetta; place 2 slices of Volpi Bresaola on top. Carefully spread 1 piece of honeycomb on bruschetta and move to serving dish. Crumble the ricotta salata over top of each and finish with a light sprinkle of orange zest.

Ricotta and Ricotta Salata

Ricotta is a moist and soft cheese, closer in consistency to a dense cottage cheese than a hard asiago. It is used as a stuffing or base in common Italian dishes, such as lasagna, manicotti, and cannelloni. A Sicilian specialty made from drained and dried ricotta, Ricotta Salata is hard, salty, and white, reminiscent of a dry Greek feta. More likely to be used for cooking rather than snacking, it is used in salads, stuffed into shells, and grated over pasta.

When winter's frost has buried much of the earth deep in snow, and a dusky coldness settles on the fields, the kitchen becomes the passionate heart of the family home. Firing up the oven to roast meat, heat casseroles, and bake bread staves off the winter's chill. The bold and spicy flavors of hot sopressata and hot coppa salami vanquish the icy dampness of winter evenings. The moments of bracing aroma, whether from a heady mixture of pungently spiced salami or the refreshing tang of the nomadic winter citrus, allow us to dream of the warmer days ahead.

Winter

Pappardelle with Oven-Roasted Tomato Sauce and Volpi Hot Sopressata

My mother taught me the importance of a well-stocked pantry that included a store of canned tomatoes. As a child, a treasured pastime was canning the summer's tomatoes for the long winter ahead.

Ingredients

1 pound pappardelle, fresh or dried (*see our recipe on page 84*)

12 oz oven-roasted tomato sauce (*see our recipe on page 85*)

4 oz Volpi Hot Sopressata Salami – sliced thin, ¼-inch julienne-cut

2 tsp garlic – fresh, minced

1½ Tbsp basil – fresh, chopped

2 oz extra-virgin olive oil

4 to 6 oz parmesan cheese, grated

Serves 4–6

Aglio (ahl'-yoh) – Garlic

Cooking Method

In a large sauce pot, bring salted water to a rolling boil, add pasta and cook until desired *al dente*. Remove cooked pasta from water, drain well, and hold warm. Reserve 2 cups of pasta water to finish dish.

Place 1 Tbsp olive oil in large sauté pan over medium heat. Slowly cook Volpi Hot Sopressata until rendered, crispy, and golden brown. Remove to paper towel-lined plate.

Place remaining olive oil in large sauté pan over medium heat. Once hot, add garlic; cook until golden brown. Add basil, sauce, and 4 to 6 oz of pasta water. Cook to a sauce consistency, approx. 3 minutes.

Add pasta to pan; cook for additional minute. Use reserved pasta water to adjust consistency, as necessary. Garnish with crispy Volpi Hot Sopressata and parmesan cheese.

Garlic: All Crush, No Cutting

Garlic, much like parsley, has been a staple in the Italian kitchen since ancient times. Whether added at the beginning of cooking or tossed into the pan moments before serving, garlic brings a distinctive flavor to any dish. Most garlic found in supermarkets is dried, which allows for a longer shelf life, but fresh garlic provides the headiest flavors. When it comes to cooking, crushing garlic is preferred—it breaks down the membranes and releases the pent-up seasoning and scents. For roasting, leave the garlic cloves whole, and the tender membranes will encase the fine paste that results from cooking.

Minestrone Soup
with Volpi Rotola Crostini

With its abundance of seasonal vegetables, beans, meat, and pasta or rice, minestrone soup brings a harvest of fond memories and an appealing defense against autumn's chill.

Ingredients

Minestrone

1 large onion, medium dice

2 stalks celery, medium dice

2 large carrots, medium dice

2 large russet potatoes – peeled, medium dice

1 Tbsp garlic – fresh, minced

¼ pound Volpi Pancetta – ¼-inch thick, small dice

½ head napa cabbage, thinly sliced

½ bunch chard, thinly sliced

3 cups spinach, rough-chopped

3 cups chicken stock

3 cups water

15 oz tomatoes, diced

15 oz cannellini beans

1 bay leaf

¼ bunch Italian parsley

3 sprigs thyme, fresh

1 sprig rosemary, fresh

1 tsp parmesan cheese per serving

sea salt to taste

black pepper to taste, freshly ground

Crostini

1 baguette, ¼-inch slices

2 oz extra-virgin olive oil

sea salt to taste

black pepper to taste, freshly ground

8 oz Volpi Basil Rotola or Volpi Sun-Dried Tomato Rotola, sliced thin

Serves 6–8

Sedano (say'-dah-noh) – Celery

Cooking Method

Crostini Preparation

Preheat oven to 350° F. Place a single layer of baguette slices on a sheet pan. Drizzle olive oil over each of the slices; season with salt and pepper. Cook until toasted and golden brown, 5 to 7 minutes. Just before serving, place a thin slice of Volpi Rotola on crostini, place in oven for 1 to 2 minutes to weep cheese.

Minestrone Preparation

Place olive oil in a large heavy-gauge stock pot over medium-high heat. Once oil is hot, add Volpi Pancetta and allow rendering and caramelizing for 3 or 4 minutes. Add onion, celery, and carrot and cook until the vegetables are *al dente*. Next, add the potatoes, cannellini beans, napa cabbage, chard, tomatoes, chicken stock, water, and fresh herbs. Stir to make sure all is blended well, and bring soup to a boil. Reduce heat and simmer for 20 to 25 minutes. Lightly season minestrone with salt and pepper. Adjust again just before serving.

To finish minestrone, add spinach and mix well. Adjust seasonings as necessary. To serve, ladle into bowls and add light grate of parmesan cheese. Garnish with Volpi Rotola Crostini.

On a Roll with Rotola

Italian for "small wheel," rotola is a subtle balance of flavors spun together in a roll for easy slicing. Volpi was first to market this gourmet treat in the United States. Rotola combinations can be deliciously witty, with creamy mozzarella, prosciutto, fresh basil, and smoky sun-dried tomatoes, or surprisingly fiery, with mozzarella and sun-dried tomatoes offset by the sizzling kick of hot salami. Rotola is admirably versatile, terrific as a snack, a pizza topping, or a great complement to your favorite entrée.

Volpi Mortadella and Potatoes
with Baked Eggs

No doubt everyone finds satisfaction in a lazy weekend brunch. This robust mixture of Volpi Mortadella, potatoes, and eggs provides an hearty start to any day.

Ingredients

1½ pounds Volpi Mortadella, ½-inch dice
5 large russet potatoes, ½-inch dice
½ cup onion, small dice
½ cup red bell pepper, small dice
6 extra-large eggs
4 Tbsp extra-virgin olive oil
2 Tbsp butter, unsalted
1 Tbsp Italian parsley, chopped
½ cup parmesan cheese, freshly grated
sea salt to taste
black pepper to taste, freshly ground

Serves 4–6

Patata (pah-tah'-tah) – Potato

Cooking Method

Preheat oven to 375° F. Place potatoes in cold, well-salted water over medium-high heat and bring to a boil. Reduce to a simmer and cook 8 to 10 minutes. Drain well and place on sheet pan. Allow to cool.

Place the Volpi Mortadella in mixing bowl. Add diced potatoes and mix well.

Preheat a large cast-iron skillet or non-stick sauté pan over medium-high heat. Once pan is hot, add olive oil and butter, then add potatoes and Volpi Mortadella to the pan in a single layer. Lower heat to medium, season with salt and pepper, and cook until golden brown. Stir occasionally, 8 to 10 minutes.

Add onions and red bell peppers. Cook until tender and onions translucent, approx. 5 minutes.

Remove pan from heat. Crack eggs gently into the pan, careful not to break the yolks. Season each with salt and pepper. Place pan in the oven and bake until eggs reach desired consistency. Remove from oven, sprinkle with parmesan cheese and parsley.

Mortadella: The Unfamiliar in the Familiar

A signature cold cut with origins in Bologna, Italy, mortadella has a more complex flavor than the bologna traditionally served in the United States. Made of finely ground pork, its distinctive look and flavor comes from the high-quality pork fat and pistachios that dot its creamy surface. All the ingredients are combined in a casing and then slowly roasted for up to 24 hours, making mortadella one of the rare Volpi products that has been cooked instead of cured.

Sautéed Prawns with Citrus Salad

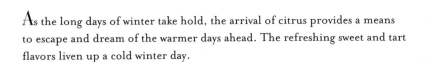

As the long days of winter take hold, the arrival of citrus provides a means to escape and dream of the warmer days ahead. The refreshing sweet and tart flavors liven up a cold winter day.

Ingredients

16 each jumbo prawns – peeled and deveined
4 Tbsp extra-virgin olive oil
1 orange
1 grapefruit
1 blood orange
1 tangerine
½ fennel bulb, thin julienne-cut
4 cups arugula
4 oz Volpi Prosciutto, ¼-inch julienne-strips
2 Tbsp butter, unsalted
sea salt to taste
black pepper to taste, freshly ground

Serves 4

Gambero (gam'-bay-roh) – Prawn

Cooking Method

Preheat oven to 400° F. Place butter in a large sauté pan over medium-low heat. Place Volpi Prosciutto in pan until rendered, crisp, and golden brown; remove to paper towel-lined plate.

Place 2 Tbsp olive oil in a large sauté pan over medium-high heat. Season with salt and pepper. Place prawns in sauté pan and cook for 2 minutes. Turn prawns; place in oven for 2 to 3 minutes to finish cooking. Remove from pan to plate with Volpi Prosciutto; allow to cool.

Citrus Salad Preparation

Remove the skin from the citrus fruits. Segment the fruit over a bowl capturing all the juices; drop the segments into the bowl as they are cut. Add the fennel and season with salt and pepper.

To Serve

When ready to serve, add arugula to the citrus mixture and mix well. Check seasoning; adjust as necessary. Divide the citrus mixture evenly between serving plates. Top each salad with 4 prawns; garnish with crispy Volpi Prosciutto.

Volpi History  Early 1980s

Uno, the building housing the Volpi operation for more than 70 years, was renovated in the 1970s to reflect the changing nature of the business, which had grown significantly under Armando's leadership. Armando's determination to apply new technology and equipment, while always protecting tradition and excellence, prompted his decision to expand. The familiar storefront and fragrant curing rooms remained intact, and the new state-of-the-art facility helped meet growing worldwide demand for Volpi products.

Volpi Stromboli

My mother is the baker in the family and the inspiration behind this recipe, which started with a young son's desire for an afternoon snack.

Ingredients

1 loaf bread dough, frozen – thawed
1½ cups crimini mushrooms, sliced
½ cup red bell pepper, julienne-cut
2 Tbsp butter, unsalted
¼ pound Volpi Capocolla
¼ pound sliced Volpi Pepperoni, very thin
¼ pound sliced Volpi Filzette Salami
¼ pound sliced Volpi Genova Salami
¼ pound sliced provolone cheese

Serves 6

Impasto (eem-pahs'-toh) – Bread

Cooking Method

Melt butter over high heat in large sauté pan. Add mushrooms, toss quickly, and let cook for 2 to 3 minutes without stirring. Once mushrooms begin to caramelize, season with salt and pepper. Toss; cook for additional 3 to 4 minutes. Once golden brown, add bell peppers. Allow peppers to cook until tender, approx. 5 minutes. Remove from heat; cool.

Place bread dough on non-stick sheet pan. Spread evenly with hands or rolling pin to create a rectangular shape, approx. 14 by 8 inches. Lay out horizontally.

Down the center of dough, neatly layer the Volpi meats horizontally. Place the mushroom and pepper mixture on top of the meats. Cover with provolone.

Lay the dough out lengthwise and perpendicular to your body. Using a sharp knife, find the center of the bread lengthwise and make a cut on each side of the bread, approx. 2 inches in length toward the middle of the dough. In each half, make another three cuts of the same length and equidistant apart. Now, on each side, there are seven 2-inch cuts.

Working left to right, take one strip of the dough and fold towards the middle to cover the filling. Next, take the strip on the opposite side and fold toward the middle, placing it on top of the first strip of folded dough. Continue this process all the way down the loaf, creating a braided appearance. The ends should fold upwards.

Preheat oven to 350° F. Cover with a towel and allow to rise, approx. 1½ hours, to double in size. Bake for 45 minutes or until golden brown. Remove from oven, brush with favorite olive oil, and allow to cool slightly.

Making the Case for Casings

Natural casings have been used for centuries to hold salami's tightly compacted ground pork. Made of animal organs, natural casings allow salami to breathe. Collagen casings provide consistency that their natural counterparts do not. The captured collagen, which comes from the middle corium layer in cowhides, is manufactured into a high-quality, thin casing that is uniform in size and strength. Although Volpi uses mainly collagen casings, the company holds true to tradition in using the original intestinal casings as well.

Bracciole with Creamy Polenta

One of my best friends in life, now an executive chef in New York City, shared this recipe with me when we were young cooks in Napa Valley. It remains a favorite in our home.

Ingredients

12 pieces bottom-round beef, sliced ¼-inch

24 slices Volpi Hot Coppa

¼ cup extra-virgin olive oil

6 Tbsp butter

8 Tbsp parmesan cheese, grated

4 cloves garlic — fresh, minced

1 cup bread crumbs

½ cup Italian parsley — fresh, minced

¼ cup basil — fresh, minced

4 hard-boiled eggs, rough-chopped

1 Tbsp capers, drained

1½ cup red wine

4 cups marinara sauce

5 cups polenta

toothpicks

For our Creamy Polenta recipe, see the Everyday Dishes section on page 87.

Serves 6

Buongustaio (bwon-goose-tay ' -eeoh) – Gourmet

Cooking Method

Pre-heat oven to 325° F. Place 2 Tbsp olive oil and butter in small sauté pan over low heat. Once butter has melted, remove and allow to cool.

On a large countertop or cutting board, place beef between sheets of plastic wrap. Using a meat tenderizer, pound beef pieces until $^1/_8$-inch thick. Use olive oil / butter mixture to baste each side of the beef. Season with salt and pepper.

In medium bowl, combine parmesan cheese, garlic, bread crumbs, parsley, basil, eggs, and capers. Season with salt and pepper; mix well. Lay flat. Place slices of Volpi Hot Coppa on top of the beef cutlet. Evenly divide the bread crumb mixture on top of each piece of beef. Spread evenly and allow a small gap around the edges. Carefully roll each piece of meat into a tight cylinder and secure with toothpick.

In large Dutch oven, over medium-high heat, add olive oil. Sear each side of the beef rolls in small batches until well-browned. Bring heat to high; add red wine to deglaze pan. Add marinara sauce, stir. Gently place each of the beef rolls back into the pan and bring to a boil. Cover pan and place in oven to finish cooking, approx. 2 hours or until fork-tender.

Deglazing for Flavor

Deglazing—the process of stripping *fond* (French for "bottom") from a pan— creates an exuberant, flavorful liquid from the mix of juices and bits of meat seared on the bottom of a pan or Dutch oven. By bringing heat to high, and adding red wine, stock, or water, the fond is easily scraped loose with a wooden spoon. After the fond is floating in the mixture, turn down the heat and strain the pieces. This dusky liquid can be used as a foundation for a spectacular sauce or gravy.

Armando Pasetti's Braised Rabbit

Armando created this dish and often serves it with polenta. When he does, he makes sure there's extra sauce to satisfy both the polenta and his dinner guests.

Ingredients

2 3-pound whole rabbits (*see how to cut up a rabbit on page 75*)
½ oz dried porcini mushrooms
1 small yellow onion, peeled and finely chopped
1 clove garlic, peeled and minced
2 Tbsp parsley — fresh, chopped
½ tsp dried oregano
2 whole cloves
¼ cup extra-virgin olive oil
¼ cup balsamic vinegar
1 bay leaf
salt to taste
black pepper to taste, freshly ground
1 cup dry white wine
1 cup chicken stock

For our Creamy Polenta recipe, see the Everyday Dishes section on page 87.

Serves 6–8

Coniglio (koh-neel'-yoh) — Rabbit

Cooking Method

Place mushrooms in a small bowl; cover with warm water and soak until soft, approx. 30 minutes. Remove and finely chop. Transfer mushrooms to a large, non-reactive bowl; add onions, garlic, parsley, oregano, cloves, oil, vinegar, and bay leaf. Season with salt and pepper. Mix well. Add rabbit pieces and rub with marinade. Cover with plastic wrap and refrigerate overnight.

Heat large skillet over medium-high heat. Add rabbit with marinade and sauté until meat is brown on all sides, 5 to 10 minutes. Add wine and cook until alcohol has evaporated, approx. 2 minutes. Stir with a wooden spoon, scraping any brown bits from bottom of pan.

Add chicken stock and bring to a simmer. Reduce heat to medium-low. Cover and cook, turning pieces occasionally, until rabbit is just cooked through and tender but not dry, 30 to 40 minutes. Uncover and continue cooking until sauce thickens slightly, 5 to 10 minutes. Remove bay leaf. Adjust seasonings as necessary. If desired, serve with polenta. See page 87 for classic polenta recipe.

How to Cut Up a Rabbit

Rabbit is a delightful meat, and a whole rabbit—weighing approx. 3 pounds—can efficiently serve up to four or five people. Look for these signs of freshness when buying: flexible front legs, fairly white meat, although the forequarters are a darker red, and a fluffy plumpness. To prepare rabbit, lay each one on its back. Using a sharp knife, cut off hind legs at the joint, near the backbone. Cut under shoulder blades to remove forelegs from rib cage. Trim off rib cage on either side of loin and discard, then trim neck and tail ends of loin and discard. Cut loin crosswise (through the backbone) into 2 to 3 pieces.

Oven-Roasted Fennel with Brown Butter and Volpi Calabrese Salami

The spicy flavor of the Volpi Calabrese Salami provides a nice kick here, making this a great accessory to braised, grilled, and roasted meats.

Ingredients

2 medium fennel bulbs – trimmed; cut each half into thirds
3 Tbsp butter, unsalted
1 Tbsp extra-virgin olive oil
8 oz Volpi Calabrese Salami
sea salt to taste
black pepper to taste, freshly ground
2 to 3 oz parmesan cheese, grated
1 Tbsp Italian parsley, fresh

Serves 4–6

Gusto (goo´-stoh) – Sense of taste

Cooking Method

Preheat oven to 375° F. Place butter and olive oil in a large sauté pan over medium-high heat. Season fennel pieces with salt and pepper. Once butter has melted, add fennel and cook for 2 to 3 minutes. Turn fennel to allow for proper caramelization. Add Volpi Calabrese Salami and place in oven to finish cooking, approx. 10 minutes.

When fennel is tender, remove from oven and sprinkle liberally with parmesan cheese. Return to oven for 1 minute to melt cheese.

Place the fennel on a large serving platter and spoon the pan juices over each piece. Garnish with parsley and serve.

Volpi History  Late 1980s

Volpi welcomed its third generation of family members into the business with the arrival of Lorenza Pasetti, Armando's daughter. Lorenza joined her father in the day-to-day operations of the company, learning firsthand the traditions of this centuries-old trade. Volpi refocused its product offerings during this period, harkening back to its authentic Italian roots by using recipes and flavors from the Old Country and by emphasizing time-honored dry-curing practices.

Gnocchi with Caramelized Mushrooms and Volpi Pancetta Sauce

One of my first cooking lessons with my son was making gnocchi: me, a three-year-old boy, and a pile of flour on the kitchen table made for a fun afternoon!

Ingredients

¼ pound crimini mushrooms, small dice
¼ pound shittake mushrooms, small dice
¼ pound chanterelle mushrooms, small dice
¼ pound portabella mushrooms, small dice
½ pound Volpi Pancetta
1 small onion, small dice
2 tsp garlic – fresh, minced
½ cup chicken stock
2 Tbsp butter, unsalted
4 Tbsp extra-virgin olive oil
2 tsp thyme – fresh, chopped
sea salt to taste
black pepper to taste, freshly ground
2 oz parmesan cheese, grated
1 Tbsp Italian parsley – fresh, chopped
1 pound fresh potato gnocchi

Visit the Volpi website (volpifoods.com) for our recipe for house-made gnocchi.

Serves 6

Fungo (foong ́-gho) – Mushroom; dried mushrooms are funghi secchi

Cooking Method

Place 2 Tbsp olive oil and Volpi Pancetta in a large sauté pan and set to medium heat. Cook to render fat from Volpi Pancetta; allow to caramelize and turn golden brown. Remove for pan and place on paper towel to drain.

In the same sauté pan, add remaining olive oil and turn heat to high. Add mushrooms to pan in batches and in a single layer. Toss once, then let sit to allow proper cooking and caramelizing. Season with salt and pepper. As mushrooms cook and shrink their size, add remaining mushrooms to the pan.

Once all mushrooms are caramelized, add onion and cook until translucent and soft, approx. 3 minutes. Add garlic; cook for 1 minute. Add thyme and cooked Volpi Pancetta. Toss to mix well. Add chicken stock and bring to a simmer, reduce heat, and cook for 2 minutes. While sauce cooks, prepare the gnocchi per directions. Add butter to sauté pan to finish sauce.

Drop the cooked gnocchi into the sauté pan; toss to incorporate. Divide evenly between serving plates. Garnish with parsley and parmesan cheese.

A Dash of Sea Salt

Salt is the most widely used ingredient in cooking, nurturing both sweet and savory flavors in the kitchen. An essential element in curing meat, it efficiently removes moisture from meat and preserves flesh. Salt also tenderizes meat and concentrates flavors. Sea salt has a different flavor than rock salt, which comes from underground mines. Produced by evaporation—natural or artificial—in ponds along a living sea or ocean, sea salt has a flaky texture. It is considered healthier than table salt because it has less sodium in its makeup. The grains come in coarse, fine, and extra fine.

Pan-Seared Halibut with Puttanesca Sauce

Made originally as a pasta dish, the bold and spicy flavor profile of this sauce complements fish as well as roasted or grilled vegetables.

Ingredients

4 6 oz halibut fillets

1½ cups tomato sauce

1 Tbsp capers, chopped

½ cup kalamata olives, pitted and chopped

½ cup green olives – pitted and chopped

½ cup tomatoes, diced

½ cup red wine

2 tsp anchovy paste

1½ tsp crushed red chili flakes

2 tsp garlic – fresh, minced

3 Tbsp extra-virgin olive oil

2 Tbsp Italian parsley

3 Tbsp basil – fresh, julienne-cut

½ cup Volpi Romano Salami – thinly sliced, julienne-cut

sea salt to taste

black pepper to taste, freshly ground

Serves 4

Cappero (kahp'-pay-roh) – Caper

Cooking Method

Preheat oven to 400° F. In a medium sauce pot add 1½ Tbsp olive oil and place over medium-high heat. Add garlic; cook until caramelized and golden brown. Add anchovy paste, capers, and olives. Cook for 30 seconds. Add red wine to deglaze pan. Add tomato sauce, tomatoes, and chili flakes. Mix well and bring to a boil. Reduce heat to low; simmer for 5 minutes.

In a large sauté pan add remaining olive oil and place over high heat. Season the halibut with salt and pepper. Once pan is hot, add halibut, presentation-side down. Cook for 2 to 3 minutes until crust is golden brown. Turn; place sauté pan in oven. Cook for 3 to 4 minutes or to individual taste.

Remove from oven. To finish the sauce, add parsley and stir. Spoon sauce over halibut and garnish with fresh basil and Volpi Romano Salami.

Our History  1990s

John Volpi and Company expanded its global footprint and its products during this time. Volpi preserved the company's catalog of dry-cured meats while offering new products such as Volpi Rotola. It also revised its label to better serve the needs of its customers. These years were marked with constant improvements in the equipment used to mature the meats, ensuring that the Old World traditions of dry curing were maintained, while enhancing the quality of the products.

The foundation for any meal's success is often found in its most basic element—the everyday dish. Profoundly simple yet essential, these ingredients are the building blocks for all our meals. Their simplicity belies their importance, as does their complementary nature. They never eclipse but rather harmonize with the exotic or powerfully flavorful components of any course. These dishes find their way into everyday life as the comfort food of childhood or the trusted culinary companions of a magnificent meal.

Everyday Dishes

House-Made Pasta – Pappardelle

Ingredients

1 Tbsp extra-virgin olive oil
2 extra-large eggs
$\frac{1}{8}$ tsp sea salt, fine
1 cup flour
$\frac{1}{2}$ cup semolina flour

Serves 3–4

Cooking Method

Place eggs, olive oil, and salt in the bowl of stand mixer. Using the paddle attachment, mix on low speed until well-blended. Combine both flours in small bowl; blend well. On low speed, add flour mix to the wet ingredients.

Remove the dough from the mixer bowl and shape into a ball. On a lightly floured surface, knead pasta dough until a smooth texture is achieved. Flatten dough to a 2-inch thickness and wrap with plastic wrap. Allow to rest at least 30 minutes.

Using a rolling pin or traditional hand crank pasta machine, cut the pasta dough into 6 equal pieces. Beginning at the widest setting, roll out dough until the desired thickness is achieved. If you're not sure, use dry fettuccini as a guideline for your thickness.

Place the sheet of pasta on a lightly floured surface. Using a chef's knife, cut into 1-inch wide ribbons. A light dusting of semolina will prevent sticking until you're ready to cook. Cook in well-salted, rapidly boiling water until *al dente*, 6 to 8 minutes.

House-Made Oven-Roasted Tomato Sauce

Ingredients

6 pounds whole pear tomatoes, hand-crushed

½ cup assorted olives – pitted and rough-chopped

6 oz extra-virgin olive oil

1 Tbsp thyme, fresh

1 Tbsp sea salt

1½ tsp black pepper, freshly ground

½ small red onion, thinly sliced

Yields approx. 1 quart

Cooking Method

Preheat oven to 250° to 275° F. Place whole tomatoes in mixing bowl; crush gently with your hands. The tomatoes should maintain some shape. Add remaining ingredients and mix together well.

Pour mixture into deep baking dish. Place in oven and allow to slow-roast until the mixture becomes dry, approx. 6 hours. The slow roasting concentrates the flavors of all the ingredients. Do not mix the tomatoes during the roasting process; look for caramelized color on the top.

Once the tomatoes are cooked, remove from oven and allow to cool in pan.

House-Made Ricotta

Ingredients

1 gallon whole milk
1 quart buttermilk, high-fat
1 pint heavy cream
1 tsp sea salt

Yields approx. 4 cups

Cooking Method

In a large pot add whole milk, heavy cream, buttermilk, and salt. Place over medium-high heat and stir frequently, making sure to touch the bottom and rounded edges of the sauce pot to prevent scorching (see chef's tip below).

Check temperature with thermometer. Once 140° F is reached, turn down to medium heat. Continue cooking with little stirring. When 170° F is reached, the curds and whey separate. (The curds rise to the top; the whey is the cloudy liquid underneath.)

Remove from heat and rest for 5 to 10 minutes; do not stir. Place an extra-fine strainer or one lined with cheese cloth over a bowl. Pour mixture through strainer to capture the cheese. Allow to drain for 15 minutes, ready to serve warm. If so desired, place in container to chill before use, as the ricotta will maintain a high quality for up to 2 days.

Chef's Tip: The proteins found in the dairy will begin to coagulate between 135° to 145° F. Once this stage is reached, the risk of scorching is reduced. Only occasional stirring will be necessary after this temperature is reached.

House-Made Creamy Polenta

Ingredients

2 ½ cups chicken stock
1 cup heavy cream
½ cup polenta
½ cup semolina
⅓ cup fontina
½ cup parmesan cheese
½ tsp nutmeg
1 tsp sea salt
black pepper to taste, freshly ground

Serves 6 (Yields approx. 5 cups)

Cooking Method

In a large saucepan add chicken stock, milk or cream, salt, pepper, and nutmeg. Place over medium-high heat and bring to a simmer. Slowly add the polenta and semolina, whisking constantly to prevent the formation of lumps. Lower heat to medium and cook for additional 2 to 3 minutes, whisking as the mixture thickens.

Reduce heat to low and switch to a wooden spoon for mixing. Continue cooking until a soft and creamy texture is achieved, 20 to 25 minutes. Remove from heat, add fontina and parmesan cheese, mix well, and hold warm.

If the polenta becomes too thick, add small increments of stock until creamy texture returns.

Acknowledgments

This book would not have been possible without Mr. Armando Pasetti, whose generosity and dedication to quality has guided Volpi Foods for more than 60 years. His passion for his family and his work inspires us all.

Any endeavor this large requires a team of skilled professionals. Helping us from start to finish, and keeping the ship righted at all times, was our talented editor, Cynthia Wilcox. Our main contact at Volpi Foods was the incomparable Adisa Kalkan, who made sure all requests were answered, and on time.

The look and feel of this book is owed almost exclusively to our gifted designer Lynne Smyers of Smyers Design. Marsha Lederman added the artistry with her graceful illustrations. Thanks to all at Reedy Press for their assistance, especially Josh Stevens and Matt Heidenry.

Finally, we would like to thank Lorenza Pasetti. An exceptional business owner, Lorenza is also the most generous of friends. It was her daring that started this project, and the book is imbued with her bighearted and passionate spirit.

Personal thanks from Sarah:
I would like to thank my family, Jane and Roger Nelson, Sam Kellogg, and all the Skutars, for their love and support. I am especially grateful for my many wonderful friends, the best of cheerleaders in every adventure. Lastly, I want to thank my friend Claudia, whose faith in me has never wavered.

Personal thanks from Michael:
To my wife, Molly, and son, Bryce, it is their unconditional love and support that have provided the foundation for my success. I am grateful for the Laukert and Gyetvan families and the sacrifices they have made during the pursuit of my vocation. Michael Chiarello's drive and passion for food provided the inspiration behind my culinary career; his generous support has allowed me to learn and grow as a chef and entrepreneur.

Index of Recipes

Orecchiette with Volpi Pancetta and Chives, 10
Pappardelle with Oven-Roasted Tomato Sauce and Volpi Hot Sopressata, 62
Polenta with Wild Mushroom Bolognese, 46
Spinach Risotto with Marscapone and Volpi Bresaola, 24

Secondi

Armando Pasetti's Braised Rabbit, 74
Frittata with Volpi Coppa, Spring Onion, and Pepper, 12
Grilled Prawns Wrapped with Volpi Pancetta and Herb Vinaigrette, 18
Oven-Roasted Chicken Breast with Corn, Green Beans, and Volpi Pancetta
  Ragu, 28
Pan-Seared Halibut with Puttanesca Sauce, 80
Poached Egg with Crispy Volpi Pancetta on Pugliese with Mixed Greens
  and Blue Cheese, 4
Pork Loin Saltimbocca with Volpi Pancetta and Sweet Potato Mashers, 56
Sautéed Prawns with Citrus Salad, 68
Volpi Italian "Hero," 38
Volpi Mortadella and Potatoes with Baked Eggs, 66
Volpi Pancetta, Lettuce, and Tomato Panini, 40
Volpi Pancetta-Wrapped Salmon with Vine-Ripe Tomato and Corn Salsa, 34
Volpi Rotola Frittata, 6
Volpi Stromboli, 70

Index of Recipes by Volpi Meats

Genova Salame

Volpi Deli Antipasto Salad, 32
Volpi Italian "Hero," 38
Volpi Stromboli, 70

Hot Coppa

Bracciole with Creamy Polenta, 72

Hot Sopressata

Pappardelle with Oven-Roasted Tomato Sauce
    and Volpi Hot Sopressata, 62

Milano Salame

Volpi Italian "Hero," 38

Mortadella

Volpi Italian "Hero," 38
Volpi Mortadella and Potatoes with Baked Eggs, 66

Pancetta

Gnocchi with Caramelized Mushrooms and Volpi Pancetta Sauce, 78
Grilled Prawns Wrapped with Volpi Pancetta and Herb Vinaigrette, 18
Minestrone Soup with Volpi Rotola Crostini, 64
Oven-Roasted Acorn Squash with Crispy Volpi Pancetta, 44
Oven-Roasted Brussel Sprouts with Volpi Pancetta, 50
Oven-Roasted Chicken Breast with Corn, Green Beans, and Volpi Pancetta
    Ragu, 28
Orecchiette with Volpi Pancetta and Chives, 10
Poached Egg with Crispy Volpi Pancetta on Pugliese with Mixed Greens
    and Blue Cheese, 4
Pork Loin Saltimbocca with Volpi Pancetta and Sweet Potato Mashers, 56
Polenta with Wild Mushroom Bolognese, 46
Volpi Pancetta, Lettuce, and Tomato Panini, 40
Volpi Pancetta-Wrapped Salmon with Vine-Ripe Tomato and Corn Salsa, 34

Pepperoni

Volpi Deli Antipasto Salad, 32
Volpi Stromboli, 70

Prosciutto

Bruschetta with Volpi Prosciutto and Fig, 58
Fettuccine with Fava Beans and House-Made Ricotta, 14
Fresh Pappardelle with Spring Peas and Volpi Prosciutto, 16
Grilled Peaches with Volpi Prosciutto and Balsamic Glaze, 22
Grilled Radicchio with Volpi Prosciutto Vinaigrette, 52
Roasted Asparagus and Volpi Prosciutto with Pine Nut Gremolata, 8
Sautéed Prawns with Citrus Salad, 68
Stuffed Baked Cherry Tomatoes, 26
Volpi Italian "Hero," 38

Romano Salame

Pan-Seared Halibut with Puttanesca Sauce, 80

Rotola

Volpi Rotola Frittata, 6

Sopressata

Volpi Italian "Hero," 38

Sun-Dried Tomato Rotola

Minestrone Soup with Volpi Rotola Crostini, 64

Armando Pasetti (left) and friends, circa 1945.

Volpi's renown for superior quality and innovative products has grown through the years, prompting the company to expand beyond Uno into new production facilities—Due and Tre.

Uno's wooden curing rooms host pancetta, coppa, bresaola, and natural-casing salami, while the renovated Due is the Volpi prosciuttoficio, housing all of Volpi's prosciutto-curing facilities. Across the street from Due, Tre is where the majority of Volpi's salami is made as well as the popular rotola.

The passing of time and tradition continued in 2002 when Lorenza Pasetti became president of Volpi Foods, and today Lorenza's children—the fourth generation of Volpi and Pasetti family members to take their place at Volpi Foods—work beside their mother and grandfather. Armando remains a steadfast, daily presence in the company, providing guidance to Lorenza and the entire staff and handing down the traditions he learned so long ago from his Uncles John and Gino.

Un Mondo™
Salami from around the World

Bringing the World to Your Table

Our shared passion for food unites us the world over.

Un Mondo brings you fine meats from Italy, France and Spain—using their traditional spice combinations and curing methods—so you can experience a world of culinary adventure in your very own home.

Try all 10 varieties of Un Mondo's distinctive international salami and sausages:

Fuet
Chorizo
Cacciatore
Herb-de-Provence

Saucisson Sec al Cepes
Saucisson Sec Al Noix
Dry Salsiccia

Dolce
Paesano
Piccante

To order these uniquely original international meat products, search for Un Mondo at **ditalia.com**.

While our culinary vision is global, our commitment to community is local.
A percentage of the sales of Un Mondo products benefit
The Moog Center for Deaf Education (moogcenter.org) in St. Louis.